ERNIE BALL GUITAR EASY CHORDS

SPEED DEVELOPERS give your fingers
DEXTERITY, STRENGTH, and CONFIDENCE.

PROPER TECHNIQUE is thoroughly explained and illustrated.

Seldom taught INITIAL MOVES slash hours of practice time by revealing
the quickest and most efficient ways to change from one chord to another.

Special THEORY SUPPLEMENTS provide a solid platform for understanding
HOW CHORDS PROGRESS and also how to change from one key to another.

Carefully graded songs like SCARBOROUGH FAIR, WABASH CANNONBALL,
and SLOOP JOHN B. demonstrate how to use the chords you learn.

THREE-CHORD TUNE LIST shows over 200 rock, pop, country, and sacred
songs that can be played using the THREE BASIC CHORDS of any key.

PLUS...

THE BLUES-world's most popular chord progression and greatest "ear" trainer.

Easiest step-by-step approach to the mean ol' F CHORD.

Doubling your range and versatility with a CAPO.

FANCY STRUMS for that professional sound.

CHORDS

CARE OF YOUR GUITAR

**CARRYING THE GUITAR
WHEN OUT OF ITS CASE:**

One hand holds the neck

Other hand under the body

Hold the neck STRAIGHT UP

**CARRYING IT
WRONG CAN:**

Break things

Hurt someone

Damage the guitar

Knock it out of tune

AVOID:

Moisture

Extreme heat

Direct sunlight

Little monsters

WASH YOUR HANDS before playing and wipe
strings clean afterwards to prolong string life.

TUNING THE GUITAR

The best way is to purchase an electronic tuner, which
allows you to tune by sight and with extreme accuracy.
No experience is required.
See your music dealer for full information.

There are many other ways to tune a guitar: With a tuning whistle, by comparing
to the pitch of another instrument, or using string harmonics. These methods all
require ear training which can be taught by your teacher or a musician friend.
Remember, the more carefully you handle your guitar the better it will stay in tune.

SITTING POSITIONS

YOUR LEG FITS INTO THE BOTTOM CURVE OF THE GUITAR BODY.

OVER RIGHT LEG   LEGS CROSSED   OVER LEFT LEG

CHOOSE THE POSITION MOST COMFORTABLE FOR YOU.

THE RIGHT HAND

Curl your
FIRST FINGER.

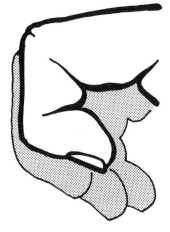

Place the pick over
the FIRST BONE
of the first finger.

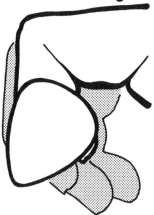

Cover half of the pick
with the FIRST BONE
of the thumb.

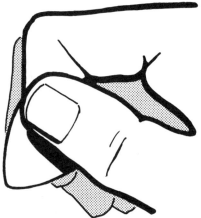

Half of the pick should be sticking out.
Hold it securely, but not too tightly.

COMMON BAD TENDENCIES

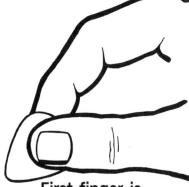

First finger is
extended too far.
Should be curled.

Pick is held by
second bones.
Use FIRST BONES!

RIGHT ARM POSITION

Scoot back into the chair and lean forward slightly.

The forearm rests on the edge of the guitar (just below the elbow).

Elbow hanging down.

NOT SO GOOD

TRY STRUMMING WITH YOUR WRIST RELAXED AND BENT.
(Pretend you are shaking water off your hand)

GO! Right hand only  / / / / / / / / KEEP IT UP...

Each slash indicates a strum.

PARTS OF YOUR GUITAR

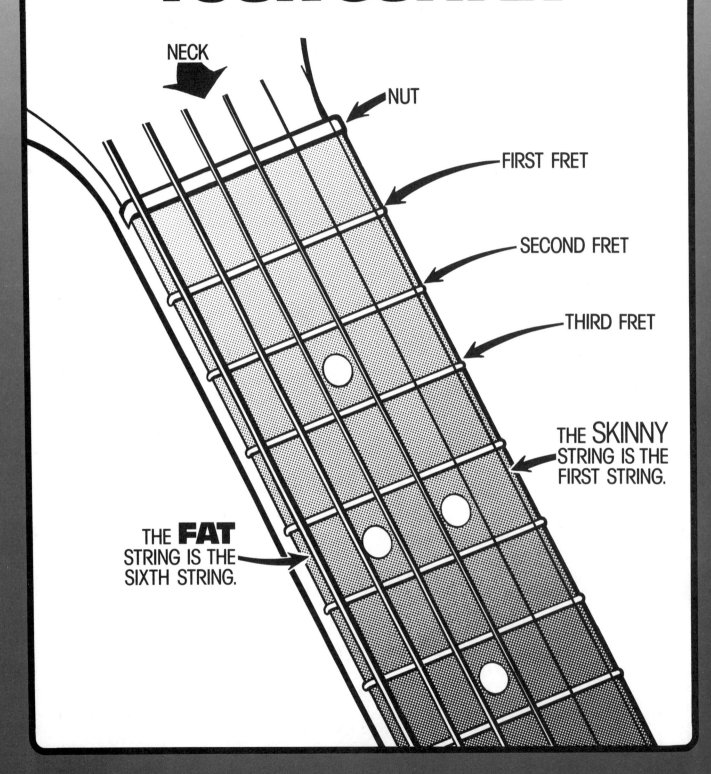

THE LEFT HAND

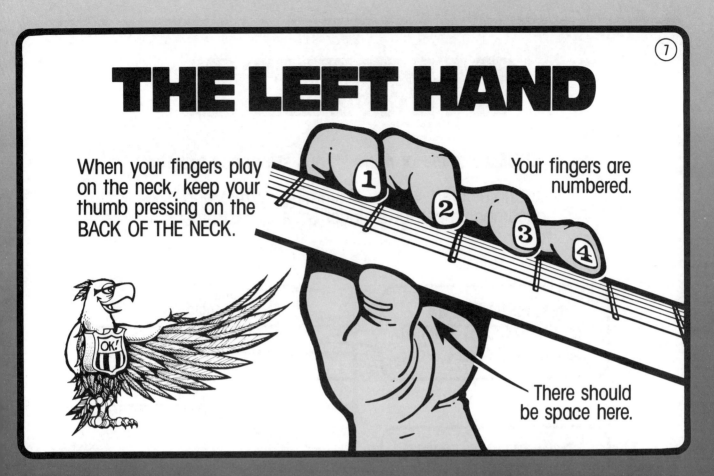

When your fingers play on the neck, keep your thumb pressing on the BACK OF THE NECK.

Your fingers are numbered.

There should be space here.

COMMON BAD TENDENCIES

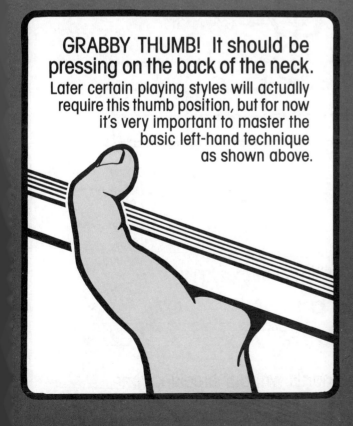

GRABBY THUMB! It should be pressing on the back of the neck. Later certain playing styles will actually require this thumb position, but for now it's very important to master the basic left-hand technique as shown above.

COLLAPSED THUMB! Should be tipped up and pressing on back.

CHORDS

A **CHORD** is three or more strings strummed together.

Chords are used for strumming rhythm and accompaniment for a singer or other instrument.

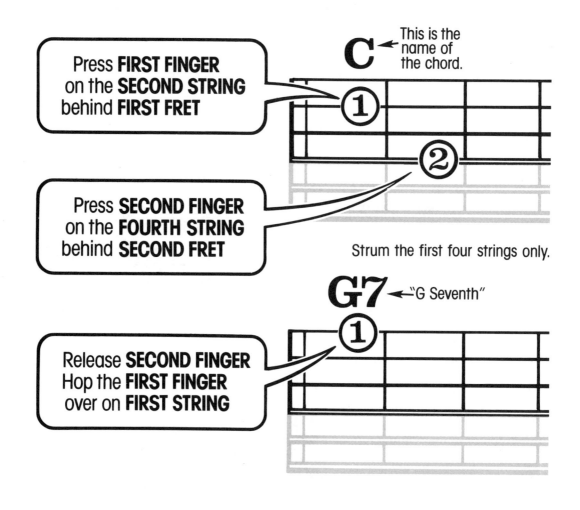

Press **FIRST FINGER** on the **SECOND STRING** behind **FIRST FRET**

Press **SECOND FINGER** on the **FOURTH STRING** behind **SECOND FRET**

C ← This is the name of the chord.

Strum the first four strings only.

G7 ← "G Seventh"

Release **SECOND FINGER** Hop the **FIRST FINGER** over on **FIRST STRING**

Play: Strum the first four (skinny) strings only.

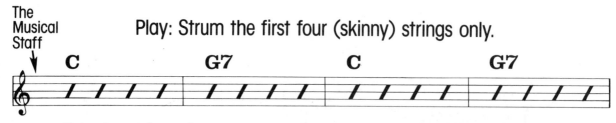

The Musical Staff

C   G7   C   G7

Practice this until you can change chords without breaking time.

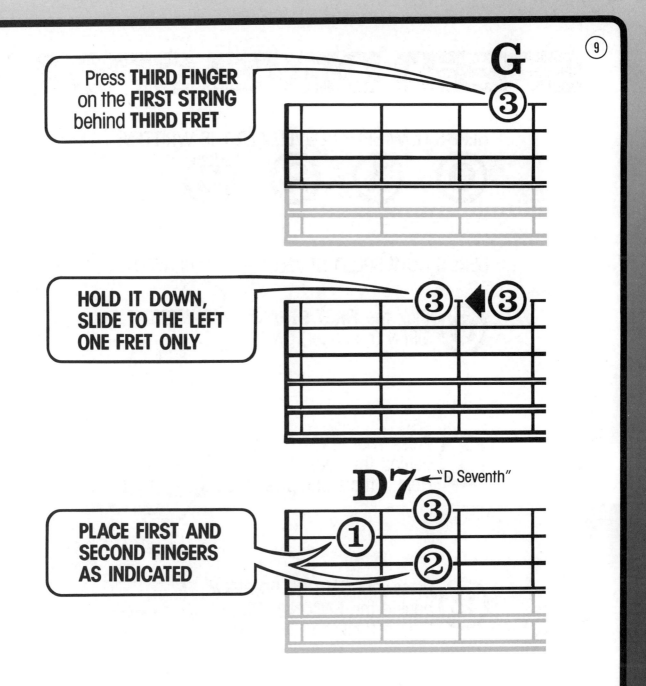

Press **THIRD FINGER** on the **FIRST STRING** behind **THIRD FRET**

G ③

HOLD IT DOWN, SLIDE TO THE LEFT ONE FRET ONLY

③ ◄ ③

D7 ←"D Seventh"

PLACE FIRST AND SECOND FINGERS AS INDICATED

① ② ③

Play: Strum the first four (skinny) strings only.

G   D7   G   D7

Practice this until you can change chords without breaking time.

Speed is not important right now! Work for a steady, even beat.

SPEED DEVELOPER 1

HERE'S HOW SPEED DEVELOPER 1 IS WRITTEN:

HERE'S HOW SPEED DEVELOPER 1 IS PLAYED:

⓪ Pick the **FIRST STRING** OPEN (no finger) ONCE.

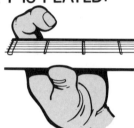

① Press your **FIRST FINGER** behind the **FIRST FRET.** Hold it there and pick ONCE.

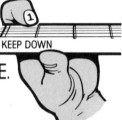

② Press your **SECOND FINGER** behind the **SECOND FRET.** Hold it there and pick ONCE.

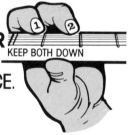

③ Press your **THIRD FINGER** behind the **THIRD FRET.** Hold it there and pick ONCE.

 DO IT 2 TIMES ON THE FIRST STRING...
DO IT 2 TIMES ON THE SECOND STRING...
DO IT 2 TIMES EACH ON THE REST OF THE STRINGS.

Speed Developers also give your fingers: **STRENGTH** to press down without tiring, **ACCURACY** to place your fingers in precisely the correct position, **DEXTERITY** to move easily from one position to another in a coordinated manner—all while achieving the best possible tone and eliminating string buzz.

**PRESS WITH YOUR THUMB
ON THE BACK OF THE NECK.**

PRESS ON THE TIPS OF YOUR FINGERS.

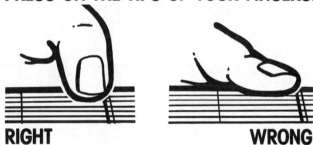

RIGHT   **WRONG**

**PLAY IT SLOWLY AT FIRST, BEING CERTAIN TO
PLACE THE FINGERS ACCURATELY IN POSITION.**

**TRY NOT TO BREAK TEMPO WHEN
SHIFTING TO THE NEXT STRING.**

**EACH DAY WORK ON INCREASING YOUR SPEED, AND AT
THE SAME TIME BE SURE TO MAINTAIN AN EVEN TEMPO.**

*Tempo = rate of speed.

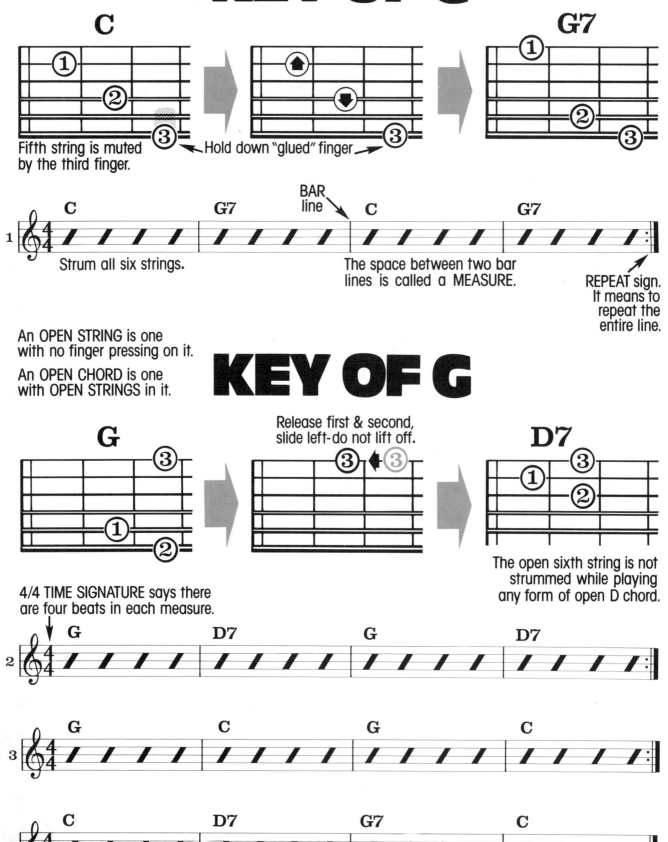

13

INITIAL MOVES

Learning to change from one chord to another need not be a frustrating experience if you remember the **4 INITIAL MOVES!** These moves will apply to ALL chord changes, no matter how advanced your guitar studies become. The FOUR MOVES are very simple, and using them enables your fingers to play as a coordinated team, resulting in smooth, flowing progressions:

GLUED FINGER

A finger that doesn't move. See opposite page.

SLIDE FINGER

A finger that slides on the same string.
See opposite page.

LIFT & SHIFT

Two fingers are lifted, holding their original position,
and then moved to a new location. See page 19.

SCOUT FINGER

None of the above applies, so one particular finger
makes the first move to a new position. It's usually the
finger that will press the lowest bass string. See next page.

THE KEY

PITCH is how high or how low music sounds.
The **KEY** determines the **PITCH** at which a song is played.
If you sing in a key that's too high or too low for your voice,
you will want to try a different key that is more comfortable.

An alphabet letter all by itself indicates a MAJOR chord or key. Guitarists usually omit "Major". (So D Major is just called "D".)

KEY OF D

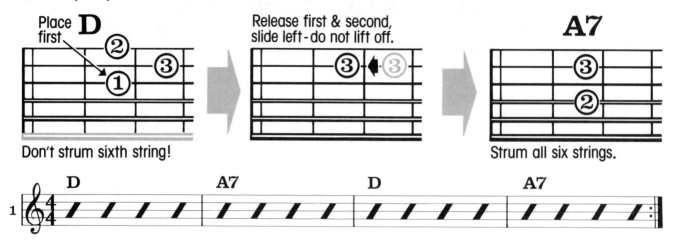

Don't strum sixth string!

Release first & second, slide left - do not lift off.

Strum all six strings.

A **CHORD PROGRESSION** is a series of chords played in a particular sequence. Many progressions are considered "stock" because they'll fit into lots of different songs. All the chord exercises throughout this book are short, stock progressions. As you practice them, keep in mind that you're learning bits and pieces that will fit right into your favorite songs later on.

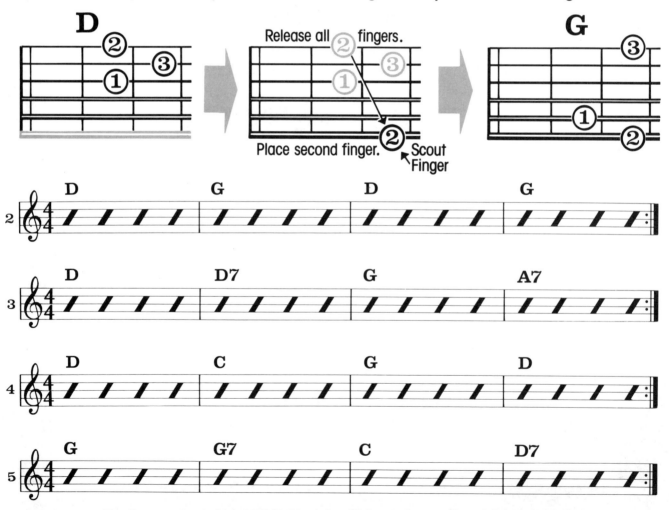

Try these progressions in 3/4 time also (3 beats in a measure instead of 4).

THE TWO BASIC CHORDS

IN EACH KEY THERE ARE TWO BASIC CHORDS. ONE OF THEM HAS THE SAME NAME AS THE KEY.

EXAMPLES:

In the Key of **C** one of the two basic chords is **C**

In the Key of **G** one of the two basic chords is **G**

In the Key of **D** one of the two basic chords is **D**

In the Key of **A** one of the two basic chords is **A**

THE OTHER CHORD IS A SEVENTH CHORD AND IT'S CALLED THE "DOMINANT SEVENTH".

To find the name of this chord, start with the name of the key. Call the "key chord" **1**, and count up the alphabet until you reach **5**.

EXAMPLE: Key of C.......**C** **D** **E** **F** **G7**
(1) (2) (3) (4) (5)

So, the other basic chord in the Key of C is G-SEVENTH

The musical alphabet uses only A through G, so after G start the alphabet all over again:

A B C D E F G **A B C**, etc.

WRITE IN THE TWO BASIC CHORDS:

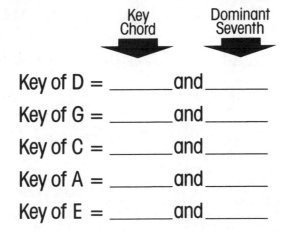

Key Chord → Dominant Seventh →

Key of D = _____ and _____

Key of G = _____ and _____

Key of C = _____ and _____

Key of A = _____ and _____

Key of E = _____ and _____

TWO-CHORD TUNES

A "TWO-CHORD" TUNE USES ONLY THE TWO BASIC CHORDS.
Pick a key and start this song, strumming the **KEY CHORD.**
Strum one time for every word-syllable and slash mark.
Change to the Dominant Seventh chord on the first **BOLD** word.
On the next **BOLD** word, change back to the **KEY CHORD.**
Each time you come to a bold word, change chords.

Down in the Valley

Melody cue:

Down in the val /* / ley / / val ley so **LOW** / / / / /

Late in the eve / / ning / / hear the wind **BLOW** / / / / /

Hear the wind blow / / love / / hear the wind **BLOW** / / / / /

Late in the eve / / ning / / hear the wind **BLOW** / / / / /

Rose es love sun / / shine / / vi' lets love **DEW** / / / / /

An gels in heav / / en / / know I love **YOU** / / / / /

Send me a let / / ter / / send it by **MAIL** / / / / /

Send it in care / / of / / Bir ming ham **JAIL** / / / / /

Bir ming ham jail / / love / / Bir ming ham **JAIL** / / / / /

Send it in care / / of / / Bir ming ham **JAIL** / / / / /

*INSTRUCTOR'S NOTE: A slash indicates a strum, the value of a quarter note. It is used when no word is sung, or when the voice is sustaining a word. The slashes are there to help maintain proper meter. When a word is divided into syllables (Bir ming ham), each syllable receives one strum, the value of a quarter note. If your student is not familiar with a song, be sure to demonstrate and participate by singing or playing the melody.

KEY OF A

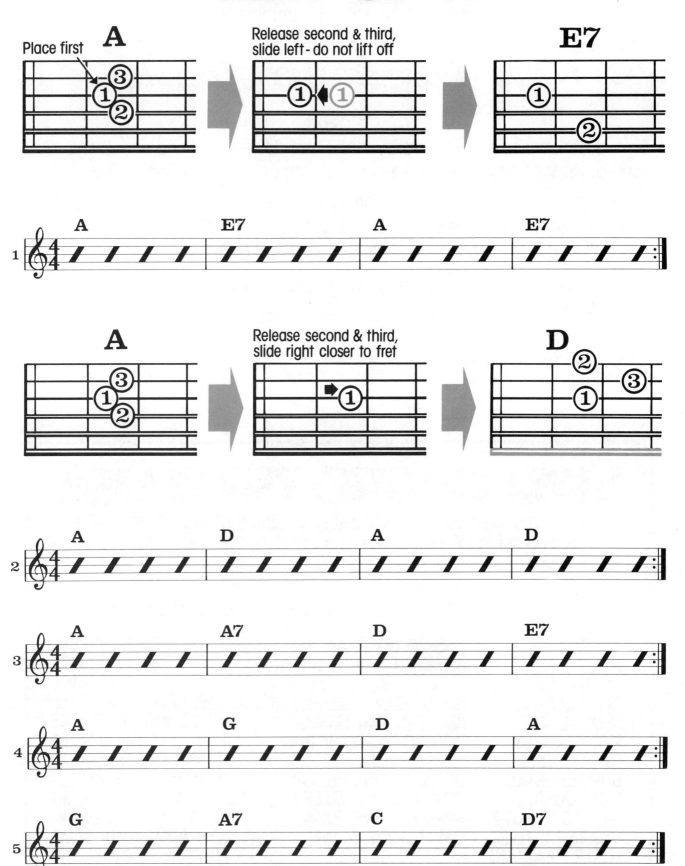

Tom Dooley

Pick a key and start the song, strumming the **KEY CHORD**.
Each time you come to a **BOLD** word, change chords.

Melody cue:

CHORUS:

Hang-down your-head Tom Doo ley / / Hang-down your-head and **CRY** / / /
Hang-down your-head Tom Doo ley / / poor-boy you're-bound to **DIE** / / /

VERSES:

1 Met her on the moun tain / / swore she'd be my **WIFE** / / /
But that gal re fused me / / there I took her **LIFE** / / / (Chorus)

2 This time / to mor row / / reck on where I'll **BE** / / /
Had n't been for gray son / / I'd-a been-in Ten nes **SEE** / / / (Chorus)

3 Bet this time to mor row / / reck on where I'll **BE** / / /
In some lone some val ley / / hangin' from-a white oak **TREE** / / / (Chorus)

TWO-CHORD TUNE LIST

Here are some tunes you can play and sing using the **TWO BASIC CHORDS**. Try your choices in all keys covered so far: C, G, D, A and E. Experiment to find the best key for your voice. Many of the songs are protected by copyright law so we didn't print the words or melodies. If you don't know the words to a song, you can find them in sheet music or from a recording.

		LITTLE KIDS' TUNES:
IDA RED	**DEEP IN THE HEART OF TEXAS**	**LONDON BRIDGE**
MEMPHIS	**BE HONEST WITH ME DEAR**	**THREE BLIND MICE**
KENTUCKY	**TAKE ME BACK TO TULSA**	**FARMER IN THE DELL**
JAMBALAYA	**MY DARLIN' CLEMENTINE**	**POLLY WOLLY DOODLE**
TOM DOOLEY	**BELL BOTTOM TROUSERS**	**HE'S GOT THE WHOLE**
RYE WHISKEY	**CONVICT AND THE ROSE**	**WORLD IN HIS HANDS**
CASEY JONES	**PISTOL PACKIN' MAMA**	**MERRILY WE ROLL ALONG**
BUFFALO GALS	**GO TELL AUNT RHODY**	**MARY HAD A LITTLE LAMB**
COCAINE BLUES	**DOWN IN THE VALLEY**	**FROGGIE WENT A-COURTIN'**
SKIP TO MY LOU	**SINGIN' IN THE RAIN**	**ROW ROW ROW YOUR BOAT**
BARBARA ALLEN	**TWO DOORS DOWN**	**SHOO FLY DON'T BOTHER ME**
LITTLE LIZA JANE	**RANCHO GRANDE**	

KEY OF E

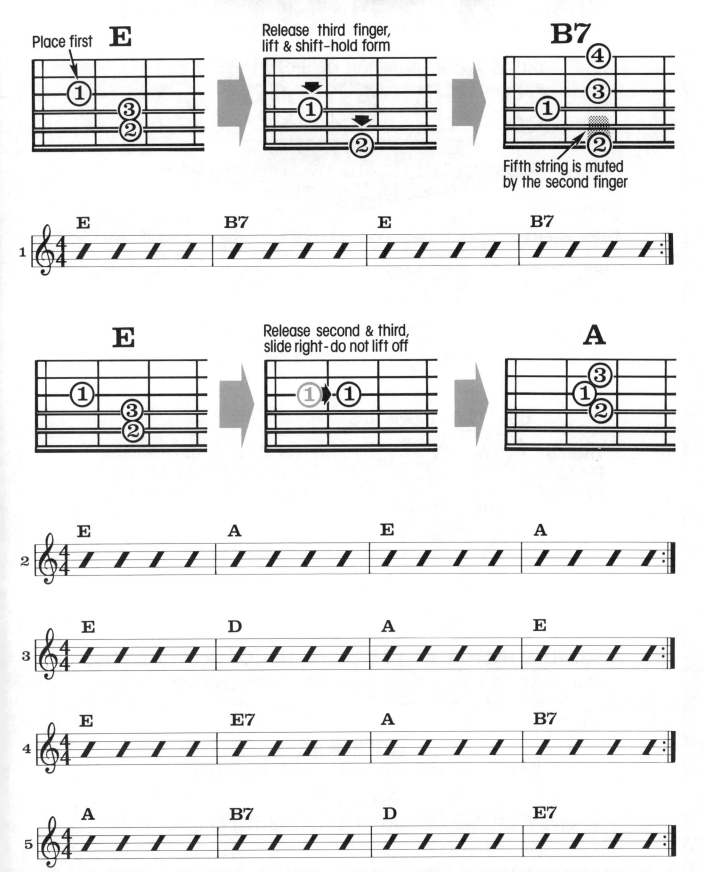

SPEED DEVELOPER 2

THIS IS A CONTINUATION OF SPEED DEVELOPER 1

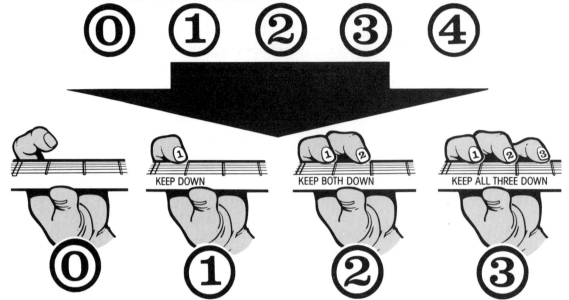

USE YOUR FINGER TIPS

THUMB PRESSED IN BACK

ALL FOUR SHOULD BE DOWN

STRETCH YOUR FOURTH FINGER SO IT PRESSES DOWN JUST BEHIND THE FOURTH FRET

SLOWLY AT FIRST—AT A NICE EVEN TEMPO—GO FOR SPEED LATER
PLAY 0 1 2 3 4 **TWO TIMES ON EACH STRING**

QUESTION:
WHY FOOL AROUND WITH SPEED DEVELOPERS?
ANSWER:
TO GIVE YOUR FINGERS DEXTERITY, STRENGTH AND CONFIDENCE!

THE THREE BASIC CHORDS

In each key the Three Basic Chords consist of the Two Basic Chords plus another called the **SUB-DOMINANT**. To find it, start with the name of the key and call it **1**. Count up the alphabet until you reach **4**.

EXAMPLE: In the Key of C......C   D   E   **F**
                                 (1) (2) (3) (4)

So **F** is the SUB-DOMINANT chord in the Key of C

WRITE IN THE THREE BASIC CHORDS:

Remember!
The musical alphabet uses only A through G, so after G start the alphabet all over again:

A B C D E F G **A B C**, etc.

	Key Chord	Sub Dominant	Dominant Seventh
Key of D =	_____	_____	_____
Key of G =	_____	_____	_____
Key of C =	_____	_____	_____
Key of A =	_____	_____	_____
Key of E =	_____	_____	_____

At this point it's beneficial to become familiar with the Three Basic Chords and how they interact with each other, which brings us to the **BLUES PROGRESSION**. More than any other, the blues progression offers the greatest opportunity to get the feel of the Three Basic Chords in operation. Professional musicians love the blues as a means of improvising, and for new players it's an enjoyable way to develop an ability to play "by ear". Even though a blues can be in any key, A and E are shown here because of their special appeal to rock, pop, folk, and country guitarists. You can play blues at any tempo,* with any beat or strumming style. Memorize the blues progression and as soon as you can play it smoothly, get together with other guitar pickers...that's when you'll have the most fun.

*Tempo = rate of speed.

BLUES PROGRESSION

Blues in A

Blues in E

CHART OF THE 3 BASIC CHORDS

KEY	Key Chord	Sub Dominant	Dominant Seventh
C	C 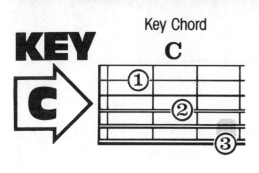	F (See page 16) 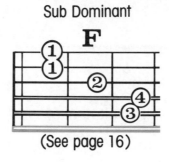	G7 
G	G 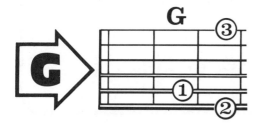	C 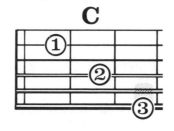	D7 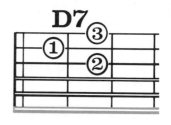
D	D 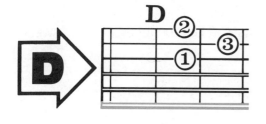	G 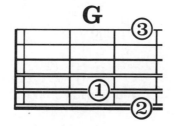	A7 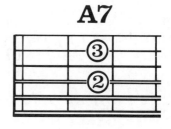
A	A 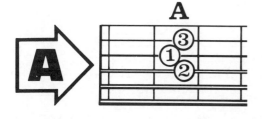	D 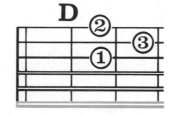	E7 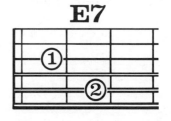
E	E 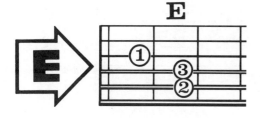	A 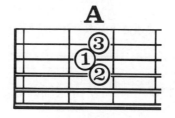	B7 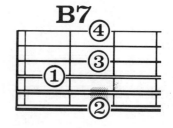

Red River Valley

Chords for the key of D are written over the words, and chords in the key of G appear underneath. One of the two keys will be more comfortable for your voice; however, practice the song in both keys in order to gain valuable experience. Play at an easy walking tempo.

CHORUS

```
D                        A7          D
Come and sit / by my side / if you love me  /  /  /  /  Do not ha / sten to bid / me a-
G                            D7          G

A7                              D        D7 (OPTIONAL) G
dieu  /  /  /   /  /  But re mem / ber the Red / Riv er Val ley  /  /  /  /  and the
D7                              G        G7            C

A7                      D
girl / that has loved / you so true  /  /  /   /  /  (Sing Verse)
D7                      G
```

```
D                        A7          D
(1) From this val / ley they say / you are go ing  /  /  /  /  We will miss / your bright eyes / and sweet
G                            D7          G

A7                          D        D7 (OPTIONAL) G
smile  /  /  /   /  /  For they say / you are tak / ing the sun shine  /  /  /  /  Which has
D7                          G        G7            C

A7                      D
bright / en'd our path / way a while  /  /  /   /  /  (Sing Verse)
D7                      G
```

```
D                        A7          D
(2) Won't you think / of the val / ley you're leav ing  /  /  /  /  Oh how lone / ly how sad / it will
G                            D7          G

A7                      D        D7 (OPTIONAL)    G
be  /  /  /   /  /  Oh / think / of the fond / heart you're break ing  /  /  /  /  the
D7                      G        G7              C

A7                          D
grief / you are caus / ing to me  /  /  /   /  /  (Sing Chorus)
D7                          G
```

SPEED DEVELOPER 3

(EL STRETCHO!)

Speed Developer 3 is the same as Speed Developer 2 except that it's played in the **5th POSITION** and no open strings are picked. 5th Position is when your **FIRST FINGER** plays on the **FIFTH FRET**.

USE ALTERNATE PICKING (down-up down-up down-up).

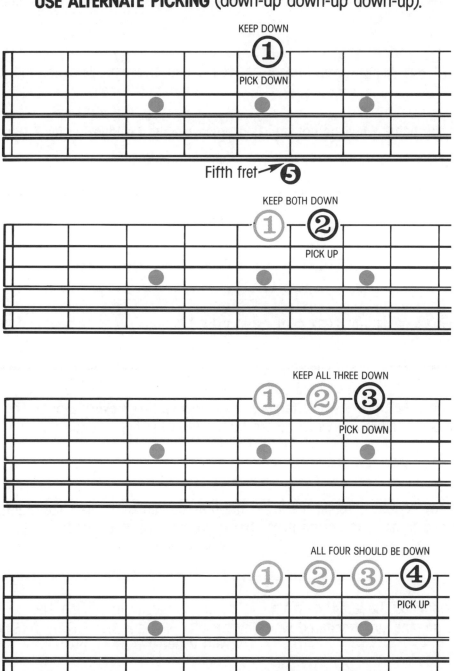

PLAY TWO TIMES ON EACH STRING.

The Blue Tail Fly

VERSES are played "out of tempo". Take your time and strum only once on each chord. Start the beat at the end of every verse, as indicated, and keep it going throughout the CHORUS.

Time to develop your memory! Chords have not been included in verses 2 thru 5. (They're the same as in verse 1.) To help you out, words are printed in **bold** type where chords change.

(1)
```
     E             A              E             B7
When I was young I used to wait on master and give him his plate, and
A             D              A             E7

E7                A            B7            E
pass the bottle when he got dry, and brush a way the Blue Tail fly / (Sing Chorus)
A7                D            E7            A
                              (with a beat)
```

CHORUS

```
E                        B7
Jimmy crack corn /-and I don't care / Jimmy crack corn /-and
A                        E7

E                                      A              B7           E
I don't care / Jimmy crack corn /-and I don't care, my mas ter's gone a way /  /
A                                      D              E7            A
```

(2) And when he'd ride in-the **afternoon**, I'd **follow** with a **hickory** broom, The **pony** being **rather** shy when **bit** ten by the **Blue** Tail fly / (Sing Chorus)
(with a beat)

(3) One day he rode a **round** the farm, The **flies** so numerous **they** did swarm, One **chanced** to bite him **on** the thigh, The **de** vil take the **Blue** Tail fly / (Sing Chorus)
(with a beat)

(4) The pony run, he **jump**, he pitch, He **threw** my master **in** a ditch, He **died** and-the jury **wondered** why, The **ver** dict was the **Blue** Tail fly / (Sing Chorus)
(with a beat)

(5) He lies beneath a **'simmon** tree, His **epitaph** is **there** to see, Be — **neath** this stone I'm **forced** to lie, The **vic** tim of a **Blue** Tail fly / (Sing Chorus)
(with a beat)

FANCY STRUMS

Time to give a little attention to your right hand. Here are a few strums along with some of the musical styles they relate to. To understand the rhythms, have a friend or teacher demonstrate. Experiment with other strums too — the right hand possibilities are limitless!

BASIC ROCK
Rock, Country Rock, Folk Rock, Blues:

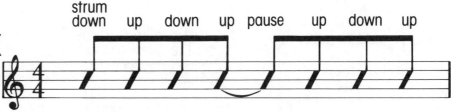

SHUFFLE
Folk Rock, Boogies, Honkey Tonk Country:

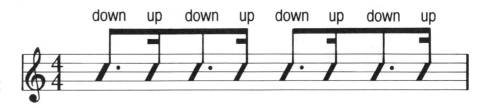

TWO-BEAT
Western Swing, Folk, Country, Dixieland:

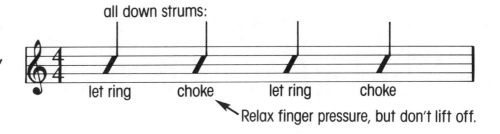

FOUR-BEAT
Big Band Swing, Jazz, Blues, Old Standards:

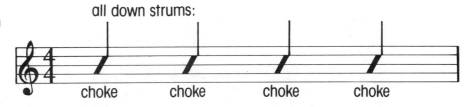

TRIPLETS
Slow Blues, 1950's, early 60's Pop (Usually slow):

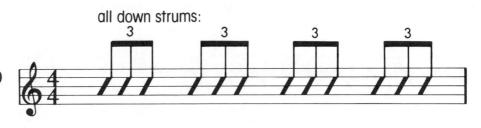

BUILDING THE F CHORD

The F CHORD, being a more advanced form, presents a unique challenge for the new guitarist. It cannot be avoided for long because it's one of the three basic chords in the key of C. We've broken down the F Chord into four learning steps. Tackle them head-on, stick with it, and suddenly you will break through.

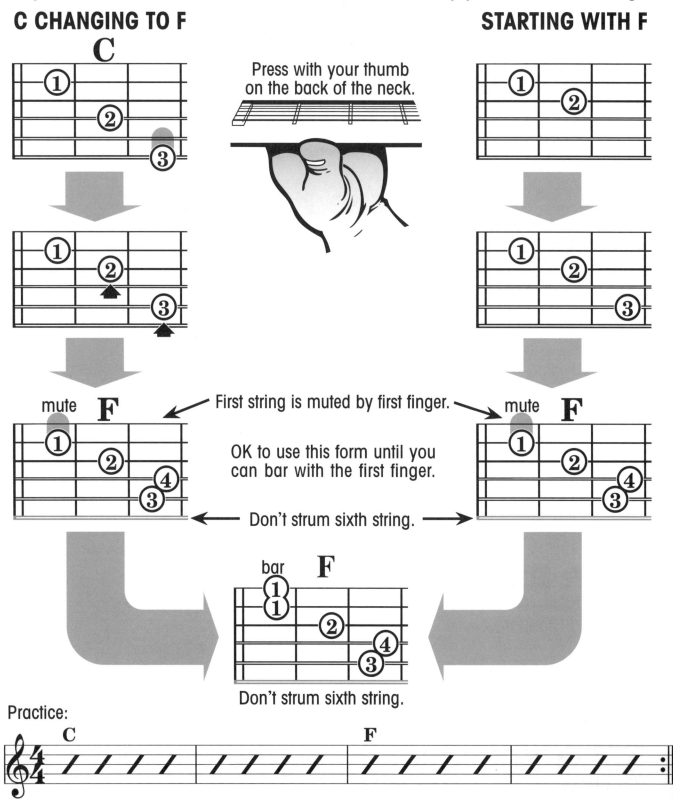

C CHANGING TO F

STARTING WITH F

Press with your thumb on the back of the neck.

First string is muted by first finger.

OK to use this form until you can bar with the first finger.

Don't strum sixth string.

Don't strum sixth string.

Practice:

Beautiful Brown Eyes

Here's an easy tune to get you started using the F chord. It's in 3/4 time, so you'll strum in groups of three. A 3/4 song is called a waltz.

CHORUS

```
C                        F
Beau ti ful beau ti ful brown eyes  /  /  /  /
G                        C

C                        G7
Beau ti ful beau ti ful brown  /  /  eyes  /  /
G                        D7

C                        F
Beau ti ful beau ti ful brown eyes  /  /  /  I'll
G                        C

G7                       C
ne ver love blue eyes a gain  /  /  /  /  /
D7                       G
```


VERSE

```
C                  F
Wil lie my dar lin' I love you  /  /  /  /
G                  C

C                        G7
Love you with all  /  my heart  /  /  /  /  To
G                        D7

C                              F
mor row we might have been mar ried  /  /  /  / But
G                              C

G7                       C
ramb lin' has kept us a part  /  /   /  /  / (Sing Chorus)
D7                       G
```

THREE-CHORD TUNE LIST

These songs can be played using the 3 BASIC CHORDS-Key Chord, Dominant Seventh, and Sub Dominant.
The name to the right indicates an artist closely associated with the tune, but not neccessarily the writer.
★Each song with a star after it uses some variation of the blues progression.

ROCK & POP

Song	Artist
AIN'T THAT PECULIAR?	Marvin Gaye
AT MY FRONT DOOR	The Eldorados
BAD MOON RISING	Creedence Clearwater
BE BOB BA LULA★	Gene Vincent
BLOWIN' IN THE WIND	Bob Dylan
BLUE BAYOU	Linda Ronstadt
BONEY MARONEY★	Johnny Winter
BYE BYE LOVE	Everly Brothers
CECILIA	Paul Simon
CHANTILLY LACE	The Big Bopper
CHERRY PINK AND APPLE BLOSSOM WHITE	Prez Prado
COTTONFIELDS	Harry Belafonte
DA DOO RON RON	The Crystals
DELTA DAWN	(several people)
DO YOU LOVE ME?	The Contours
GAMES PEOPLE PLAY	Joe South
GIVING IT UP FOR YOUR LOVE	Delbert McClinton
GLORIA	Van Morrison
GREAT BALLS O' FIRE	Jerry Lee Lewis
GREEN DOOR★	Crystal Gayle
GUANTANAMERA	The Sandpipers
HANG ON SLOOPY	The McCoys
HEARTACHES BY THE NUMBERS	Ray Price
I DON'T WANT TO KNOW	Fleetwood Mac
I HEAR YOU KNOCKING	Fats Domino
I LIKE IT LIKE THAT	Chris Kenner
IT'S A HARD RAIN GONNA FALL	Bob Dylan
JUST LIKE A WOMAN	Bob Dylan
KANSAS CITY★	(many artists)
LAY DOWN SALLY	Eric Clapton
LONELY BOY	Paul Anka
LONELY STREET	Andy Williams
LOUIE LOUIE	Kingsmen
LOVE IS STRANGE	Nickey & Sylvia
MARY ANNE	Ian & Sylvia
MISTER TAMBOURINE MAN	Bob Dylan
MONEY★	Barrett Strong
MY ELUSIVE DREAMS	Bobby Vinton
NEW ORLEANS	Gary U.S. Bonds
PEACEFUL EASY FEELING	Eagles
PRESSURE DROP	Maytals
QUEEN OF HEARTS	Juice Newton
ROCK AND ROLL MUSIC	Beatles
ROCK AROUND THE CLOCK★	Bill Haley
SEA CRUISE	Bobby Darrin
SECOND HAND NEWS	Fleetwood Mac
SEVENTH SON	Johnny Rivers
SHANTY TOWN	Desmond Dekker
SINGIN' THE BLUES	Guy Mitchell
SLOOP JOHN B.	Beach Boys
SLOW DOWN★	Larry Williams
SMACK DAB IN THE MIDDLE	?
SPANISH HARLEM	Ben E. King
SPEEDO★	The Cadillacs
STEAM ROLLER BLUES★	James Taylor
SUMMERTIME BLUES	The Who
SURFIN' USA	Beach Boys
SWEET SURRENDER	Robert Gordon
THE GREAT PRETENDER	The Platters
THE TIDE IS HIGH	Blondie
TINY BUBBLES	Don Ho
TUMBLIN' DICE	Rolling Stones
TWIST & SHOUT	Beatles
WAKE UP LITTLE SUSIE	Everly Brothers
WAYWARD WIND	Gogie Grant
WHAT I SAY★	Ray Charles
WHOLE LOT OF SHAKIN' GOIN' ON	Jerry Lee Lewis
WOOLY BOOLY★	Sam The Sham
YACKETY YAK	The Coasters
YOUR MAMMA DON'T DANCE AND YOUR DADDY DON'T ROCK & ROLL★	Loggins & Messina
ALL SHOOK UP	Elvis Presley
BLUE SUEDE SHOES★	" "
DON'T BE CRUEL	" "
HEARTBREAK HOTEL★	" "
HOUND DOG	" "
I GOT A WOMAN	" "
IT'S ALL RIGHT MAMA★	" "
JAILHOUSE ROCK★	" "
MY BABY LEFT ME	" "
BROWN EYED HANDSOME MAN	Buddy Holly
HEART BEAT	" "
OH BOY	" "
RAVE ON★	" "
READY TEDDY★	" "
WORDS OF LOVE	" "
BACK IN THE USA★	Chuck Berry
FORTY DAYS★	" "
JOHNNY B. GOODE★	" "
MAYBELINE★	" "
NADINE★	" "
REELIN' AND A ROCKIN'★	" "
ROLL OVER BEETHOVEN★	" "
SCHOOL DAYS★	" "
TOO MUCH MONKEY BUSINESS★	" "
YOU NEVER CAN TELL	" "
GOOD GOLLY MISS MOLLY★	Little Richard
KEEP A KNOCKIN'★	" "
LONG TALL SALLY★	" "
LUCILLE★	" "
RIP IT UP★	" "
SLIPPIN' AND A SLIDIN'★	" "
TUTTI-FRUTTI★	" "
BLACK LIMOUSINE	Rolling Stones
CRAZY MAMA	" "
HONKY TONK WOMAN	" "
19th NERVOUS BREAKDOWN	" "
SATISFACTION	" "
SHE'S SO COLD	" "
START ME UP	" "

COUNTRY WESTERN

AM I THAT EASY TO FORGET?	(many artists)
ARE THE GOOD TIMES REALLY OVER?	Merle Haggard
ASHES OF LOVE	Johnny & Jack
BATTLE OF NEW ORLEANS	Jimmy Driftwood
BLUES STAY AWAY FROM ME★	(several artists)
BONAPARTE'S RETREAT	Glen Campbell
BORN TO LOSE	Ray Charles
BREAK MY MIND	Anne Murray
CIGAREETS & WHISKEY	Jack Elliot
CHAINED TO A MEMORY	Eddy Arnold
CINDY (GIT ALONG HOME)	(lotsa folks)
COAT OF MANY COLORS	Dolly Parton
COLUMBUS STOCKADE BLUES	Jimmy Davis
COOL WATER	Sons/Pioneers
COWARD OF THE COUNTY	Kenny Rogers
CRAZY ARMS	Ray Price
DANG ME	Roger Miller
DETOUR	Tex Williams
DOWN THAT WRONG ROAD AGAIN	Crystal Gayle
EACH MINUTE SEEMS/MILLION YRS	Eddy Arnold
FIRE BALL MAIL	Roy Acuff
FOGGY RIVER	Carl Smith
FOLSOM PRISON BLUES★	Johnny Cash
FOUR WALLS	Jim Reeves
FRAULEIN	Bobby Helms
GREEN GROW THE LILACS	Tex Ritter
GREEN GREEN GRASS OF HOME	(many artists)
HARPER VALLEY PTA	Jeannie C. Riley
HAVE I TOLD YOU LATELY THAT I LOVE YOU?	Gene Autry
HE'LL HAVE TO GO	Jim Reeves
HE STOPPED LOVING HER TODAY	George Jones
HUMPTY DUMPTY HEART	Hank Thompson
I BELIEVE IN YOU	Don Williams
I CAN'T STOP LOVING YOU	(many artists)
I FALL TO PIECES	Linda Ronstadt
I NEVER BEEN TO HEAVEN	?
I NEVER GO 'ROUND MIRRORS	Lefty Frizzell
I WALK THE LINE	Johnny Cash
IF DRINKING DON'T KILL ME	George Jones
IF YOU'VE GOT THE MONEY HONEY	Lefty Frizzell
I'LL SAIL MY SHIP ALONE	Ernest Tubb
I'M SO AFRAID OF LOVING U AGAIN	Charlie Pride
I'M THINKING TONIGHT OF MY BLUE EYES	Eddy Arnold
IS ANYBODY GOIN' TO SAN ANTONE	Charlie Pride
IT MAKES NO DIFFERENCE NOW	Floyd Tillman
IT'S HARD TO BE HUMBLE	Mac Davis
I'VE ALWAYS BEEN CRAZY	Waylon Jennings
JEALOUS HEART	Tex Ritter
JOLE BLON	Moon Mulligan
KING OF THE ROAD	Roger Miller
KISS AN ANGEL GOOD MORNING	Charlie Pride
LAST WORD IN LONESOME IS ME	Roger Miller
LONE STAR BEER & BOB WILLS MUSIC	Red Steagall
LOST HIGHWAY	Leon Payne
MAMAS DON'T LET YOUR BABIES GROW UP TO BE COWBOYS	Waylon & Willie
MOM AND DAD'S WALTZ	Lefty Frizzell
MOUNTAIN DEW	Grandpa Jones
MOVIN' ON★	Hank Snow
MY BABY THINKS HE'S A TRAIN	Rosanne Cash
NIGHT TRAIN TO MEMPHIS	Roy Acuff
OKIE FROM MUSKOGEE	Merle Haggard
PINS & NEEDLES IN MY HEART	Roy Acuff

PLEASE RELEASE ME	(many artists)
REMEMBER ME	T. Texas Tyler
RING OF FIRE	Johnnie Cash
ROLLIN' IN MY SWEET BABY'S ARMS	Lester Flatt
SIGNED SEALED & DELIVERED	Cowboy Copas
SIX DAYS ON THE ROAD	Dave Dudley
THAT'S HOW MUCH I LOVE YOU	Eddy Arnold
THE GAMBLER	Kenny Rogers
THE WINDOW UP ABOVE	George Jones
THIS OLD HOUSE	Stuart Hamblin
TODAY I STARTED LOVING U AGAIN	Merle Haggard
T. FOR TEXAS★	Jimmy Rodgers
TOGETHER AGAIN	Buck Owens
TONIGHT THE BOTTLE LET ME DOWN	Waylon Jennings
TRUCK DRIVIN' MAN	Conway Twitty
TWO DOLLARS IN THE JUKEBOX	Eddie Rabbit
WABASH CANNONBALL	Roy Acuff
WALKIN' AFTER MIDNIGHT	Patsy Cline
WALKIN' THE FLOOR OVER YOU	Ernest Tubb
WHEN MY BLUE MOON TURNS TO GOLD AGAIN	(several people)
WHITE LIGHTNIN'	George Jones
WHY BABY WHY	Webb Pierce
WILD SIDE OF LIFE	Freddy Fender
WORRIED MIND	Jimmy Davis
YOU ARE MY SUNSHINE	Jimmy Davis
AFTER THE FIRE IS GONE	Willie Nelson
BLUE EYES CRYIN' IN THE RAIN	" "
DEVIL IN A SLEEPING BAG	" "
LOCAL MEMORY	" "
SHOTGUN WILLIE	" "
SO MUCH TO DO	" "
WHISKEY RIVER	" "
YOU LOOK LIKE THE DEVIL IN THE MORNING	" "
COLD COLD HEART	Hank Williams
HONKY TONK BLUES★	" "
I CAN'T HELP IT IF I'M STILL IN LOVE WITH YOU	" "
I'M SO LONESOME I COULD CRY	" "
LOW DOWN BLUES	" "
MANSION ON THE HILL	" "
MAY YOU NEVER BE ALONE	" "
MIND YOUR OWN BUSINESS★	" "
MOVE IT ON OVER★	" "
THERE'LL BE NO TEARDROPS TONIGHT	" "
WEDDING BELLS	" "
YOU WIN AGAIN	" "
BUBBLES IN MY BEER	Bob Wills
BRAIN CLOUDY BLUES★	" "
CORRINE CORRINA★	" "
FADED LOVE	" "
HANG YOUR HEAD IN SHAME	" "
HOME IN SAN ANTONE	" "
I CAN'T GO ON THIS WAY	" "
KEEPER OF MY HEART	" "
MAIDEN'S PRAYER	" "
MILK COW BLUES★	" "
MISS MOLLY	" "
MY CONFESSION	" "
ROSE OF OLD PAWNEE	" "
STAY ALL NIGHT	" "
STILL WATER RUNS THE DEEPEST	" "
TIME CHANGES EVERYTHING	" "
TROUBLE IN MIND	" "

FOLK & TRADITIONAL

BEAUTIFUL BROWN EYES
BIG ROCK CANDY MOUNT'N
BLUE TAIL FLY
CARELESS LOVE
CATTLE CALL
CRAWDAD SONG
FRANKIE AND JOHNNIE
GOLDEN SLIPPERS
GOODNIGHT IRENE
GOODNIGHT LADIES
GOTTA TRAVEL ON
HAND ME DOWN MY WALKIN' CANE
HOME ON THE RANGE
JESSE JAMES
JOHN HENRY
I GAVE MY LOVE A CHERRY
LETTER EDGED IN BLACK
LITTLE BROWN JUG
MICHAEL ROW THE BOAT ASHORE
MIDNIGHT SPECIAL
ON TOP OF OLD SMOKEY
O' SUSANNA
O' THEM GOLDEN SLIPPERS
PUT ON YOUR OLD GREY BONNET
RED RIVER VALLEY
SHE'LL BE COMIN' ROUND THE MOUNTAIN
STRAWBERRY ROAN
SWANEE RIVER
THIS LAND IS YOUR LAND
WHEN THE SAINTS GO MARCHIN' IN
WORRIED MAN BLUES

SACRED & GOSPEL

AMAZING GRACE
FAITH OF OUR FATHERS
FARTHER ALONG
GLORYLAND WAY
I SAW THE LIGHT
I'LL FLY AWAY
IN THE GARDEN
JESUS LOVES ME
JUST A CLOSER WALK WITH THEE
NEARER MY GOD TO THEE
OLD RUGGED CROSS
SOFTLY AND TENDERLY
THAT OLD TIME RELIGION
WHERE COULD I GO (BUT TO THE LORD)
WILL THE CIRCLE BE UNBROKEN

MINOR CHORDS

C minor and G minor are advanced forms called Bar Chords,
so we'll work with A, D, and E minor only for the time being.

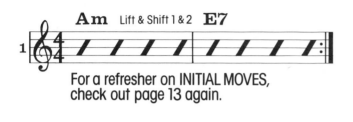

For a refresher on INITIAL MOVES,
check out page 13 again.

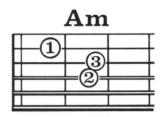

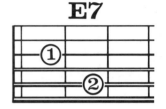

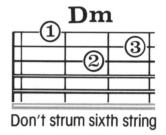

Don't strum sixth string

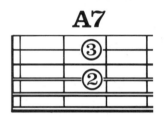

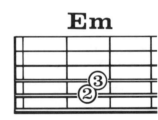

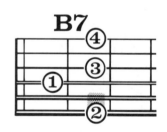

Scarborough Fair

3/4 TIME:

(1)
```
Em                  D            Em
Are / you go ing to Scar bo rough Fair? /  /  /  /  /
Am                  G            Am
```

```
G          Em           A    Em
/ Pars ley sage / rose ma ry and thyme /  /  /  / Re mem / ber
C          Am           D    Am
```

```
G                   D
me / to one that lives there /  /  /  /
C                   G
```

```
Em      D           Em
For / she was / a true love of mine /  /  /  /  /
Am      G           Am
```

(2)
```
Em                     D          Em
Tell her to make me a cam / bric shirt /  /  /  /  /
Am                     G          Am
```

```
G          Em           A    Em
/ Pars ley sage / rose ma ry and thyme /  /  /  / With out / a
C          Am           D    Am
```

```
G                     D
seam / or fine nee dle work /  /  /  /  /
C                     G
```

```
Em       D          Em
And / she'll be / a true love of mine /  /  /  /  /
Am       G          Am
```

(3)
```
Em                   D           Em
Tell her to find me an a cre of land /  /  /  /  /
Am                   G           Am
```

```
G          Em           A    Em
/ Pars ley sage / rose ma ry and thyme /  /  /  / Be tween / the
C          Am           D    Am
```

```
G              D
sea foam / and the sea sand /  /  /  /  /
C              G
```

```
Em      D             Em
Will / you plough / it with a lamb's horn /  /  /  /  / (Sing 1)
Am      G             Am
```

QUIZ

Place the correct number next to each answer:

1. OPEN _____ Time Signature indicating 4 beats in a measure.

2. PITCH _____ When a finger touches a string to prevent it from sounding.

3. TEMPO _____ The space between two bar lines.

4. BAR LINE _____ Key, Dominant Seventh, Sub-Dominant.

5. 4/4 _____ Flat.

6. MUTE _____ How high or how low music sounds.

7. MEASURE _____ Chords changing from one to another.

8. KEY _____ Time Signature indicating 3 beats in a measure.

9. 3/4 _____ Three or more strings strummed together.

10. 3 BASIC CHORDS _____ 5 lines and 4 spaces upon which music is written.

11. PROGRESSION _____ Vertical line dividing the staff.

12. MAJOR _____ A chord identified by a little m.

13. STAFF _____ Establishes the pitch of a song.

14. CHORD _____ A string with no finger pressing it down.

15. TIME SIGNATURE _____ A chord identified by a single alphabet letter (Sometimes with a flat or sharp next to it).

16. MINOR _____ How fast music is played.

17. ♭ _____ Tells how many beats in a measure.

OTHER WAYS

There's more than one way to finger certain chords. Some guitarists argue that one is better than another; but if you keep an open mind while experimenting with the choices, you'll find that either form has its advantages, depending on the situation. Here are a few examples of other ways to play some of the chords already learned. Try each option described below; knowing all the possibilities will help you become a more versatile player.

C

1. GLUED FINGER gives security for beginners changing to G7.
2. You can strum ALL six strings.
3. It's a MOVABLE form IF you mute all strings not fingered. (Try moving it up the neck.)

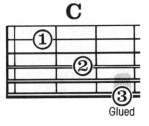
Glued

C

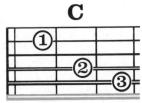

1. No glued finger, so a change to G7 requires lifting all fingers.
2. It doesn't sound very good if you strum the sixth string.
3. This is not a movable form.
4. You have TWO glued fingers when changing to F (good!).

A

1. Nice easy SLIDE over to D or E7.
2. LIFT the first finger for easy A7.
3. SLIDE first finger LEFT to the first fret and you get Amajor7. Often used in pop music. Try it.

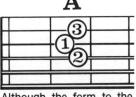
Although the form to the right is most often taught, this one is more versatile.

A

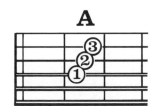

1. No easy sliding to D or E7.
2. LIFT second finger for easy A7.
3. A change to Amajor7 requires lifting all fingers and replacing.

G

1. Easier for beginners because the stronger fingers are used.
2. The change to G7 or C requires lifting all fingers and replacing.

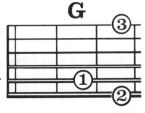

G

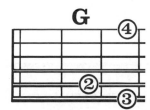

1. Not so easy for beginners because weaker fingers are used.
2. Very easy changing to G7 or C with glued fingers.
3. Now is a good time to start practicing this form.

B7

1. Easy LIFT & SHIFT to E chord.
2. OK to strum all of the strings.

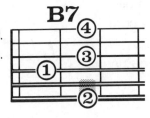

B7

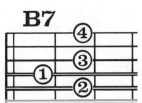

1. Second finger is glued when changing to E.
2. It doesn't sound very good if you strum the sixth string.

Sloop John B.

4/4 time, basic rock beat:

(1)
G
We came-on the-Sloop John B. / / /-my grand / father and me / / /
D

G   D7
'round / Nas sau town / we did roam / / /   / / drinkin' all
D   A7

                        OPTIONAL
G   G7   C   Am   G
night / / /   / got-into a fight / / /   / / / I feel so-broke up
D   D7   G   Em   D

D7   G
/ I-wanna go home / / /   / / / (Sing Chorus)
A7   D

CHORUS

G
So hoist-up the-John B. sails / / / See-how the-main sail sets / / /
D

G   D7
Send-for the-captain a shore / let-me go home / / /   / / let-me go
D   A7

                        OPTIONAL
G   G7   C   Am   G
home / / /   / / let-me go home / / /   / / / I feel so-broke up
D   D7   G   Em   D

D7   G
/ I-wanna go home / / /   / / / (Sing Verse)
A7   D

---

(2) The first mate he got drunk / / / broke-up the cap tain's trunk / / /
Consta ble had to come and take-him a **way** / / /   / / Sheriff John—
stone / / / / please leave-me a **lone** / / /   / / / I **feel** so-broke up
/ I-wanna go **home** / / /   / / / (Sing Chorus)

(3) The poor cook he got fits / / / Ate-up all-of the grits / / /
Then he took and threw-a way all-of the **corn** / / /   / / Sheriff John—
stone / / / / please leave-me a **lone** / / /   / / / This **is** the-worst trip
/ I-ever been **on** / / /   / / / (Sing Chorus)

Wabash Cannonball

4/4 time, country two-beat:

OPTIONAL

① E   E7
From-the great At lan tic O cean / to-the wide Pa ci fic
A   A7

A   B7
shore / / Hear-the queen of flow ing moun tains / to-the south belle by the
D   E7

OPTIONAL

E   E7
door / / She's long / tall and hand some / she's loved by one and
A   A7

A   B7   E
all / / She's-a mod ern com bi na tion called the Wa bash Can non ball / / / (Sing Chorus)
D   E7   A

CHORUS
Lis ten to the jin gle / /-the rum ble and the
roar / / / **Rid** in' thru the wood lands / to-the hill and by the
shore / / Hear-the migh ty rush of en gines / hear-the lone some ho bo
squall / / / **Rid** in' thru the jun gles on the Wa bash Can non **ball** / / (Sing Verse)

---

② Now-the east ern states are dan dies / so-the west ern peo ple
say / / From **New** York to Saint Lou is and Chi ca go by the
way / / Thru-the hills of Min ne so ta / where-the rip pling wa ters
fall / / No **chan** ces can be ta ken / on-the Wa bash Can non **ball** / / / (Sing Chorus)

③ Here's to Dad dy Clax ton / may-his name for ev er
stand / / / **Will** he be re mem bered / thru parts of all our
land / / When-his earth ly race is o ver / and-the cur tain 'round him
falls / / We'll carry him on to vic t'ry / on-the Wa bash Can non **ball** / / / (Sing Chorus)

THE CAPO

A CAPO is a device which clamps all six strings firmly down on the fretboard, thereby raising the pitch of every string.

You have studied OPEN chords in the keys of C, G, D, A, and E. Open chords have some strings that are not pressed down by your fingers.

This is a FLAT

♭

There are other keys too, such as F, B♭, E♭, A♭, and D♭, but their chords aren't open forms. To play in these keys, you can either learn new, advanced chords,* or use a capo.

A capo allows you to play in the other keys right now, utilizing the same familiar chords studied thus far. The chart on the next page shows many new chords created by capoing at the first fret.

*The sequel to this book deals with movable "bar" chords, and hopefully you'll continue into that area soon.

Key Chord	Sub Dominant	Dominant Seventh

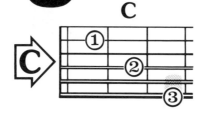 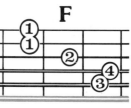 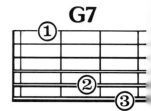
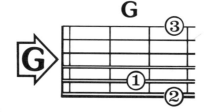 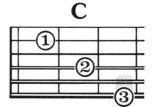 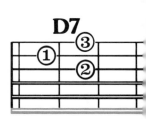
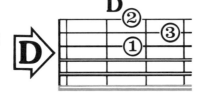 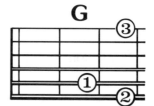 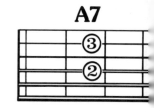
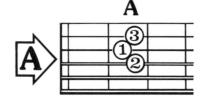 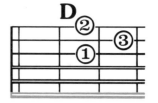 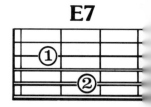
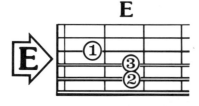 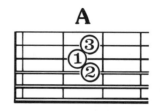 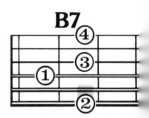

THE MINOR CHORDS

  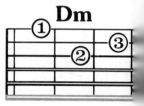

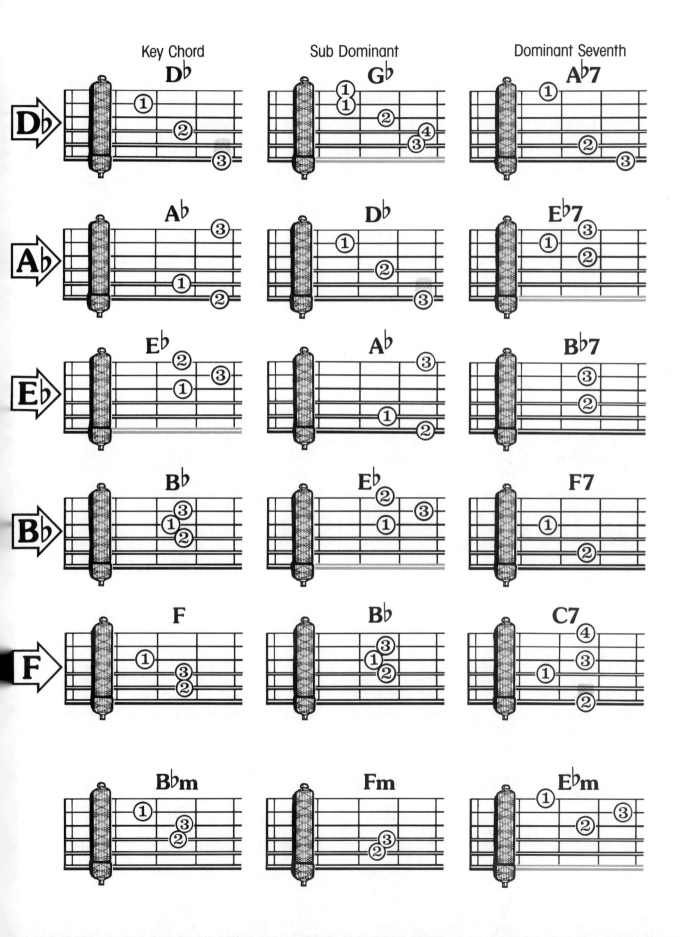